Seasonal Poetry

Kristyn Glaspy

BookLeaf Publishing

Presentation by *BookLeaf Publishing*

Web: www.bookleafpub.com

E-mail: info@bookleafpub.com

ISBN: 9789357441025

First edition 2023

To all the poets who think they can't write poetry

Life

Life is not a straight line
It is winding and flowing
It is full of walls and hedges
It forks and spoons out holes.

Life is full of choices
Choices to live or die
Choices to survive or give up
Choices to stand tall or stay down.

Life is not handed to anyone
It is stolen from some
It is swooped around to others
It even punches a few.

Life is not a straight line
But a roller coaster of decisions
All depending how you choose to live

Moon

The solemn glow of gray that spreads out along
the horizon
And along my heart. The beauty in each phase
and with each phase,
Hidden in plain sight the darker side.
Surrounded by so many
Yet close to only a few. The moon and I have
much in common for
It is the moon where I learned my ways.

The stars might call the moon a friend
But they are closer to the sun.
The Earth may say so too
But it worries only about itself.

Glowing in the dark,
The moon continues to revolve around others.
It goes through phases as I go through seasons.
We understand that we are not lonely
Nor are we alone,
But we are left out.

Caged

Have you ever thought about being a bird,
Locked behind bars, never to be free?
Looking to the outside never to fly,
Waiting for the day the doors unlock?

Being a bird is fun and games
Until you realize you are caged.
You are caged behind bars that never move
Bars that are never unlocked for you.

As a bird you wait for the golden key
To turn the lock and set you free.
You wait for the day that you can fly
Away from the world you know of now.

But when you finally find that freedom
The cage feels less like a trap.
Freedom is great for awhile
But freedom is choosing to go back.

You realize the cage was home
And that the bars were never locked.
You realize the key was never there
And that you needed to trust yourself.

Thunderstorm

Tapping against the concrete
Lighting up the sky
Booms of loud drums
Making my skin jump
A storm has come
and I am in love with it.

The Door

Don't open the door

The world slows to halt as you sweep me off my feet and I am pulled from reality.

Don't open the door

We stand in unison but not in union as my back is facing you and you grab my hand.

Don't open the door

You spin me around and I know...I know what you want but I cannot trust you.

Please don't open that door

You surprise me with an embrace, one I have been yearning for but know not to trust.

I'm begging, don't open the door

You opened the door of emotion while the front door opens to reveal our secret embrace.

The door opens

But that door, the door to my heart must remain
closed.

That door has to be locked.

Cottonwood

As the cottonwood falls from a hidden tree

I count another season passing.

Each piece of floating fluff reminds me of the
winter we have sprung out from

And when the sun sets, giving each piece a
lovely glow

I smile, breathing in a scent of summer.

Esther

"Who knows, perhaps you have come to your
position for such a time as this" Esther 4:14B

She pulls her hair behind her ear.
She can feel her heart pumping;
With every beat, she feels she cannot breathe.
She trembles as she stands at his door.
Her hands are cold and clammy.
Should she knock? Or just walk in?
Her crown is heavy on her head,
as is the shadow that hovers over her,
Warning her not to enter.
She raises her chin, giving herself courage,
It never came easy.
She pushes the doors open and with a soft
expression,
he welcomes her inside.

Love

It is not a simple reply.
It means so much more than "I love you"
It means that you are my sun,
my moon,
my stars
It means you are my galaxy
It means that you are my everything
It holds ever cheesy movie line within four
letters
It means you are the Romeo to my Juliet
The Jay Gatsby to my Daisy
The Darcy to my Elizabeth
Those four letter hold so much more
Than a simple reply

Dreams

Dreams are–sweet
Dreams are–sour
Dream can come at any hour,
Dreams are where a warning you might meet.

For some, their dreams are vivid–
The dreams take up much strength.
How much, will depend on the length
And the dreamer may wake rigid.

The sweetest dreams make worries disappear
While people and new places appear.
The sourest dream bring anxieties
Like watching one's self fall and praying for
sobriety.

Depression

You're falling down a hole,
But you are not scared.
There is a certain, familiar feeling
That this hole gives you.
It wraps around you like a blanket,
Giving a false sense of security.
You are not scared, but you're not
Calm either, you are nothing.
Just as the hole is nothing,
You feel nothing. No emotions.
You fall further and further,
Curling up into a ball, waiting
To hit the ground.
Darkness consumes you, numbness
Carries you away. The hole
Grows deeper and
Deeper and
Deeper
Until you can feel nothing else
But the weight of the world
Calling you names.

Anxiety

Like a boat on choppy water
Anxiety rocks you.
The water is dark below you,
And the clouds are dark above you.

Your stomach drops
As the waves rise.
You begin to shake
When the winds suddenly calm.

You are stuck
As the world moves around you.
The boat rocks
But you can't move.

There is no way out.
As you watch the waves grow
And feel the wind pick up
All you can do is pray.

Nothing makes sense
But every thought is in motion.

Happiness

Sunflowers always point towards the sun
And the color yellow is always fun.
If eyes are windows,
Then smiles are mirrors.

Mirrors mimic the soul
While windows can be dull.
If sunrises bring a smile,
Then I hope sunsets bring laughter.

Autumn

The sun is warm upon my skin
But there is a cool breeze coming in.
Gray clouds cover the sky
As a cold front comes from the north;
Autumn come forth
Do not let the cool wind die

From a Star

Dear moon, is it the sun you shine for at your
brightest
Or hide from at your darkest?
If I am a single star amongst
The entire universe,
then I will lend you my light to glow
even if you begin to feel low.

The Hunt

It is not about what you kill
It is about waking up at 4am knowing it will be
cold.
It is about sipping hot chocolate to keep warm
And eating a breakfast that agrees with you.
It is about watching the sun rise
And waiting for the animals that rise with it.
It is not about what you kill
But about how it all makes you feel.

Holidays

The holidays are here
People smile with cheer.
Christmas trees have gone up,
Nativities scenes have come out
And people celebrate and shout
For the New Year

Isolation

Who knows how long
These months will last.

Seasons go by
Temperatures change
Summer turns to winter

We sit in our homes
Clean as can be

Till someone comes in
Wearing nothing but a cough on their sleeve

Stuck

It is okay to feel stuck,
To feel like you can't move.
It is okay to not know what to do,
To feel like you are in a rut.
It is okay to feel stuck,
To feel like you are trapped in mud.
It is okay to feel stuck.
Feel stuck,
It is okay.

The Poor Farm

I can smell the prickly leaves
And the trees that never look the same.
The smell of the house is always the same,
It's floorboards creaking with every step,
Pushing up the old scent of rotting wood.
I can smell the wind from the East,
Bringing me the remnants
Of what used to be cows grazing,
But is now fresh wet sand and diesel.
I smell the powder that comes from corn
And the wet liquid we pour out,
Calling the deer.
I smell the wind as we race
Through the now gravel road and reach
The low waters of the trinity.
I can smell the fishy water as we cast
Our lines and wait for a bite.
The poor farm, I know it well.

Unafraid

She was unafraid
        The world was waiting for her
And she was unafraid

Home

Home is not the long brick building;
It is not the fenced in backyard
Or the U-shaped driveway.
Home is the first entrance past a large birdhouse,
It is the smell of wet sand and tall hills.
Home is that sight of ducks floating in a puddle,
It is the transition from a gravel road
To mud that will make any car or truck slide.
Home is the small brick house that holds
Long lost memories and new ones.
Home is the clubhouse that holds new inside jokes
And new company. It holds fishing poles, ammo,
Boats and buggies.
Home is the feelings of wide open fields blowing wind
That smells like corn and cotton.
Home is where my heart is.